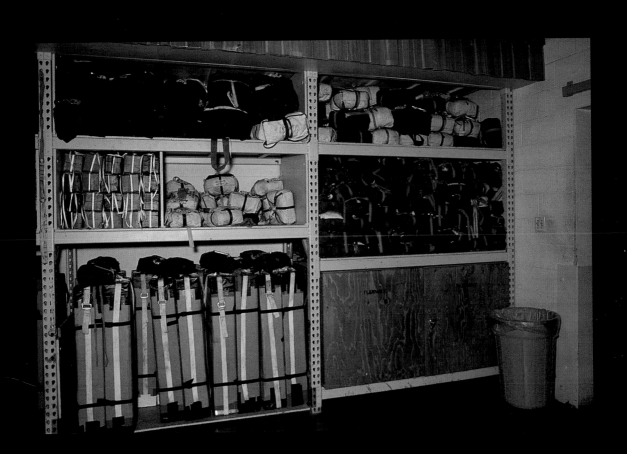

DOROTHY HINSHAW PATENT

FIRE
FRIEND OR FOE

PHOTOGRAPHS BY WILLIAM MUÑOZ
CLARION BOOKS • NEW YORK

Page 1: Cargo boxes and other equipment are packed and ready to go at the Missoula Smoke Jumpers Center.
Pages 2-3: Firefighters at work.
Page 5: Glacier lilies bloomed in the forest during the spring of 1989.
Page 6: Lush grass thrives in Yellowstone eighteen months after the fires.

Clarion Books
a Houghton Mifflin Company imprint
215 Park Avenue South, New York, NY 10003

Text copyright © 1998 by Dorothy Hinshaw Patent
Photographs copyright © 1998 by William Muñoz

The text is set in ITC Century Book

Printed in Hong Kong

Library of Congress Cataloging-in-Publication Data
Patent, Dorothy Hinshaw.
Fire : friend or foe / by Dorothy Hinshaw Patent ; photographs by William Muñoz.
p.   cm.
Summary: Discusses forest fires and the effect that they have on both people and the natural world.
ISBN 0-395-73081-3
1. Fire ecology—Juvenile literature.   [1. Forest fires.   2. Fire ecology.   3. Ecology.]   I. Muñoz, ill.
II. Title.   QH545.F5P38 1998   577.2—dc21   98-11754   CIP   AC

DNP 10 9 8 7 6 5 4 3 2 1

DESIGNED BY RACHEL SIMON

ADDITIONAL PHOTOGRAPH CREDITS
Dorothy Hinshaw Patent: pages 19, 22, 26, 48, 73
Yellowstone National Park: pages 2-3, 30, 42, 44-45, 54-55, 57, 58-59, 60
Kent Wood: page 11
Michael Gallacher: page 47

For my brother Horton.
—D.H.P.

For Ditto.
—W.M.

Contents

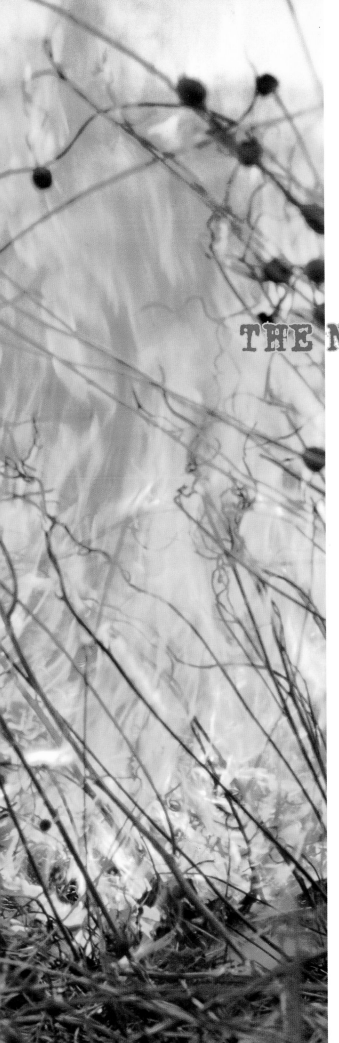

ONE

THE NATURE OF FIRE

Humans have always been fascinated by fire. This amazing process creates heat and light but can also bring death and destruction. When people figured out how to tame fire, how to start it on their own, and how to use it to improve their lives, they had taken one of the major steps toward civilization.

We love fire, but we also hate and fear it. We may be able to control fire when in our fireplace or at the tip of a candle, but in nature fire is its own boss. Every

Fire has always fascinated humans.

The yellow part of a flame consists of tiny bits of glowing soot.

Fourth of July, grass fires start from firecrackers and firework displays, sometimes burning large areas of grassland before coming under control. During dry years, forest and grassland fires caused by lightning or careless people sweep across the land, often burning houses as well as trees and grass.

What Is Fire?

Fire is unique. It isn't solid like dirt, or liquid like water. We can see it, but we can also see through it. Flames flicker and dance in yellow, orange, and blue before our eyes, never staying in the same place for long. Barbecue coals and fireplace wood glow in bright orange that pulses and shimmers.

Fire is actually a well-defined physical process, with three requirements—fuel, oxygen, and heat. When a burnable substance warms up, its molecules and their electrons move around faster and faster. When it gets hot enough, the chemicals in the fuel break down and combine with oxygen in the air, releasing a burst of heat and light. This process is called "combustion." As the heat intensifies, other chemical bonds in the burning material break,

ABOVE: Lightning is the cause of almost all natural fires.
BELOW: A tree can be quickly consumed by fire.

and the resulting fragments also combust. Thus fire feeds on itself, creating the heat necessary for the combustion of still more fuel. Unless it runs out of fuel or oxygen, a fire will continue to burn.

During combustion, fire destroys the complex chemical structure of the organic material it burns. Wood, paper, even bone, become powdery ash. But in that ash lie nutrients that help the next generation of plants grow. Nitrogen, phosphorus, potassium, and other vital elements that were locked up in the trunks of trees and the dried stems of grasses are freed and become available to fertilize new plant growth. Fire in nature also opens up forests and meadows to the sunlight from which plants gain the energy they need for growth. This combination of fertilizer and sunlight means that, soon after a fire, robust new growth begins. The roots of many plants survive fire, and these send up new shoots. Seeds germinate, and new plants grow.

LEFT: **Soon after a fire, new growth thrives.**

Young trees will take over a meadow unless fires burn regularly.

TWO
PEOPLE AND FIRE

We tend to think of humans as separate from nature. But we have always been a part of nature and have in turn influenced it ever since we came on the scene. Sometimes, our influence has altered ecosystems profoundly.

Around the world, native peoples have used fire for centuries to create an environment friendly to human activities. In what is now New England, Native Americans burned the forest floor twice a year, creating parklike woodlands with very little

Native Americans helped maintain the prairie by setting frequent fires.

Bison were the most important animals the Plains Indians hunted.

undergrowth. The lack of undergrowth made traveling through the forest much easier for hunters pursuing game. It also created the conditions that favored species they liked to hunt, such as deer, elk, and wild turkey.

Creating the Prairie

The great American prairies, grasslands that extend for hundreds of miles across the midsection of the North American continent, were also fostered by fires set by Indians. The intrusion of forest into the prairie was held in check by frequent burning of the grassland and deliberate firing of forest tracts. The Plains Indians were hunters who depended largely on the American bison (popularly called buffalo) for survival. And bison thrive on grassland. The more prairie, the more bison and other game such as elk and pronghorn. When tallgrass prairie is not burned, it eventually reverts to forest.

Stands of ponderosa are sometimes burned to thin them out.

19

Ponderosa Forests and Fire

When the conquistadores came to the American Southwest in the sixteenth century, the ponderosa pine forests that grew there were open, with well-spaced trees and tall grass. The grass burned at low intensity every few years, holding down the growth of young ponderosas and other forest trees. Older ponderosas are resistant to low level fire, so their health was unaffected.

Then, in the 1800s, cattle and sheep were introduced into the system, grazing on the grass. The government saw fire as an enemy and viewed grazing as a way to keep the grass in check, thereby eliminating the periodic fires. Fire seemed wasteful—it burned away livestock feed and killed young trees that could otherwise be allowed to grow into harvestable timber.

When cattle are allowed to overgraze, they can damage the land and cause many problems.

Grazing brought drastic changes to the landscape. Without grass, the bare ground eroded badly, and gullies up to 40 feet deep were created. Tree growth exploded. In one area, the density of ponderosas grew from an average of 23 per acre to 851 per acre. Where grassland animals like bluebirds, pronghorn, and grasshoppers once lived, forest creatures such as nuthatches, porcupines, and bark beetles multiplied.

Nowadays, fires are rare in these more dense Southwest forests. But when they come, they can be devastating. A raging fire in the Tonto National Forest in Arizona in 1990, for example, was impossible to contain and destroyed houses and trailer parks as well as killing six firefighters. Such fires wreak havoc not only on humans, but can also kill more than 95 percent of the trees, destroying the forest almost completely and setting it back hundreds of years.

This tropical forest in Costa Rica has not been burned or grazed.

Slashing and Burning

Cutting down forests to create pasture and cropland is an ancient human tradition. In various forms, similar methods have been used around the world to replace forests with land for domesticated animals and crop plants. At the beginning of the dry season, trees in the selected area are killed by cutting off branches and ringing the bark (destroying part of it in a circle all around the tree), which disrupts the flow of water and nutrients within the tree. The dead trees dry out, and as the rainy season approaches, fires are set to burn the vegetation. Slash and burn achieves two goals at once. First, the ground is cleared of vegetation. Second, the ash from the burning trees and brush provides valuable fertilizer for pasture or crops. After a few years, grazing or crop growing exhausts the fertilizer, and the farmers clear new areas of forest.

When human populations were small and the wild world was large, slash and burn agriculture wasn't too destructive. Eventually, forests bordering the treeless areas took over again. But as the human population grew, it overwhelmed the forests. Today, this ancient technique, along with clear-cut logging, is rapidly depleting the great rain forests that span the equator and help regulate the world's weather.

THREE

Fire came to Earth long before living things, so it's no surprise that both plants and animals have ways of dealing with this powerful natural force. Living things are not helpless before fire.

Each kind of natural environment, or ecosystem, has its own rhythms with relationship to fire. While it's natural for grasslands to burn every few years, the lodgepole pine forests of Yellowstone National Park burn every 250 to 350 years.

Ten years ago, fire burned the forest where these healthy young trees are now growing.

25

Redwoods can live for hundreds of years, surviving many fires along the way.

Plant Adaptations

Long-lived trees, such as ponderosa pines and redwoods, have thick, fire-resistant bark. A giant sequoia redwood can have bark a foot thick. In an ancient redwood grove, many of the trees are scarred by fires that occurred dozens to hundreds of years ago. Trees like these are rarely killed by fire, which is one reason they manage to live for so long.

Other species, such as the lodgepole pine, are adapted to rare,

These young aspen shoots, recognizable by their yellow autumn leaves, are growing to replace the mature tree killed by fire.

devastating fires like those in Yellowstone in 1988. The lodgepole burns easily when dry, but it produces two kinds of cones. One kind opens by itself and contains seeds that sprout during years when there are no fires. The other type of cone is held shut by sticky resin. These fire-resistant cones, called serotinous cones, do not open in an ordinary year. When a hot fire roars through a lodgepole forest, it kills almost all the mature trees. But the heat from the fire also melts the resin that protects the serotinous cones, opening them. Once the seeds are released, they will germinate and grow into the next generation of lodgepoles. Other trees, such as the jack pine of the North and the Baker cypress, which lives in Northwestern forests, also have serotinous cones. Many shrubs also have seeds that require fire to germinate, which can lie dormant for decades awaiting a burn.

The longleaf pine, which lives in the American Southeast, has its own unique way of dealing with fire. Low intensity fires on the forest floor, which could kill small seedling trees, burn frequently in the longleaf pine forests. Instead of sprouting as a seedling tree, the young longleaf grows like a clump of grass for several years, protecting the growing tip in the center. After the young plant has developed deep roots, the longleaf sends up a strong, fast-

Fireweed.

growing shoot that carries the vulnerable growing tip quickly above the danger zone.

Aspen trees live in areas with moist soil, such as along creeks or near underground springs. Each clump of trees actually arises from the same roots. Aspen are adapted to periodic fire, which kills the old trees in a clump that may have been damaged by very cold winters or insects. The clump is rejuvenated by fire when healthy new growth sprouts after the old growth is killed off. If the clump goes too long without fire, its health can be weakened by having no young vigorous growth.

Grasses are especially well adapted to fire. The growing point, or crown, of grass lies at the surface of the ground, where it is

Lupine, like fireweed, thrives after fire.

protected from fire that sweeps quickly through the dry grass. The roots of grasses penetrate deeply into the soil and easily survive a normal fire.

Many wildflowers thrive after fires that open up the ground to sunlight. The underground stems of fireweed are protected from burning, and it flourishes after a fire, blooming with bright pink flowers. Its dandelion-like seeds are also scattered by the wind into burned areas, where they sprout into vigorous plants.

Winners and Losers

A burning fire can harm or benefit animals. Hunters, such as hawks and coyotes, are attracted to its edges, where they feed on small animals like mice that are fleeing the fire. Insect-eating birds, too, often feed around a fire as their prey is forced to fly. Many animals, such as prairie dogs and ground squirrels, are hardly affected. They simply burrow into the ground to wait out the fire. The popular image of frightened deer racing to escape a forest fire as portrayed in the movie *Bambi* is false. Deer and large grazers, such as elk and bison, will feed right near the edge of a fire. If a fire becomes very intense, they can easily outrun the flames.

Even a huge fire doesn't faze grazers like this bison crossing the road during the Yellowstone fires.

Pronghorn are grassland animals that can outrun the fastest fire.

FOUR
AFTER THE BURN

The first rainfall after a fire brings a rapid flush of green. During the spring after the Yellowstone fires of 1988, tiny lodgepole seedlings, surrounded by the blackened trunks of their dead parents, were already stretching their shoots upward toward the abundant sunlight. Joining the pines were twenty kinds of grasses as well as wildflowers such as glacier lilies and shooting stars.

A young pine seedling growing in 1991.

35

Some birds, like this pileated woodpecker, feed on insects that attack dead trees. They also make their nest holes in such trees.

Return of the Birds

Fire may destroy the homes of some birds, but it provides new homes for others. The burned Yellowstone forests rang with the *rat-a-tat-tat* of woodpeckers feeding on bark beetles and making nest holes where they could raise their young. Warblers and sparrows increased in numbers because they prefer the varied landscape left in the aftermath of fire to the dark and closed mature lodgepole forest. But birds such as goshawks, which need the old growth, retreat into the untouched stands of trees that remain after fire. Their numbers may decrease until the mature forest returns.

Changes over the Years

Every ecosystem has its own timeline, changing with the years after a major event such as a fire. The first plants to grow are those that are resistant to fire and resprout from their roots and also those whose seeds lie dormant, waiting for the stimulus of fire to germinate. These plants are sun lovers, sending up flourishing growth with the stimulation of open space and nutrients in the ashes.

Fast-growing shrubs accompany the grasses and wildflowers, as do young trees. Over the years, the shrubs and trees shade out the sun, and some of the plants that grew quickly after the fire, such as fireweed, disappear. In a few more years, the trees grow tall enough to shade the shrubs, and they decline as well.

As the plant species change, so do the animals. Grazers like elk thrive in the burned-over forest on the nutritious new plant growth, and birds feed on insects that specialize on those same plants. Ground nesters, like meadowlarks, and birds that nest in

holes in dead trees, such as bluebirds and woodpeckers, are also common in burned-over areas.

By the time the forest is mature again, much of the animal life is gone. With reduced sunlight to fuel plant growth under the trees, there is little food for insects, so insect-eating birds are few. Dead trees fall and block the forest floor, making it difficult for large animals to get around. A mature lodgepole pine forest, for example, is a place of little life other than the pine trees themselves. The deadwood and weaker, old trees provide the perfect fuel, awaiting a dry year, another fire, and another cycle of renewal.

ABOVE: **Lush grass thrives in Yellowstone eighteen months after the fires.** BELOW: **Elk love to graze on fresh green grass.**

FIVE

FIGHTING FIRE

Fire continues to shape the American West today. Even though millions of people live in the western states, many millions of acres of grassland and forest are still unpopulated public land vulnerable to burning. Even in populated areas, every few years, grassland fires in California burn out of control and destroy homes. The burning is a part of nature in an area with a weather cycle of wet and dry seasons rather than the four seasons. In much of California, it's normal for no rain to fall for several months. Combine the

Dry grass catches fire easily.

41

Grass fires burn quickly, so they don't heat up the ground excessively.

dryness with extreme heat and winds, and a simple spark from a discarded cigarette or a hot catalytic converter on a car can cause a furious grass fire.

Western forests, too, are prone to fire. After a couple of dry years, trees can be low in moisture content and burn easily. A wet spring, during which shrubs grow rapidly, followed by a hot, dry summer can also spell disaster. The heavy undergrowth can carry a fire through a forest. Forest managers have no choice but to deal with forest fires in some way.

Modern firefighters have many weapons for fighting wildfires when necessary. Satellite communications enable fires to be pinpointed, even when they occur deep in forested wilderness. Space-age materials protect firefighters from flames and heat, and helicopters and airplanes can drop water, fire-retardant chemicals, and smoke jumpers who parachute in to help put out fires.

Lines of Defense

When fires occur near roads, getting firefighters to the scene is easy. The first line of defense against a fire is to create a fuel break. Without fuel, a fire can't burn. So firefighters work hard to create a line that fire can't cross. They use their heavy axes, called pulaskis, to cut down trees and shrubs and to dig into the ground, breaking up surface vegetation to slow the fire. Firefighters concentrate their work downwind of the fire, in the direction the fire is moving most quickly.

The firefighter on the right is using the hoe end of his pulaski.

Many fires can be limited by encircling them with a firebreak. But some fires burn too hot or too fast to be stopped by a few feet of bare ground. To halt these fires, firefighters set a backfire. A backfire burns the area in front of a wildfire, depriving the wildfire of fuel. Backfires can be tricky. If the wind changes, a backfire itself can burn out of control. During the 1988 Yellowstone fires, a backfire threatened the town of Cooke City, Montana, just outside the park.

Firefighters at work.

The Firefighter's Equipment

Modern science helps protect firefighters in their dangerous work. Their clothing is made of Nomex, a material that won't burn or melt even at seven hundred to eight hundred degrees Fahrenheit. When it gets that hot, the Nomex forms a charred material that still offers some protection to its wearer. Firefighters wear gloves made of flame-resistant leather and chaps made of nylon on

the outside and Kevlar, a tough material also used for bulletproof vests, on the inside. This combination protects firefighters from both the flames and the sharp saw blades they use to cut down trees.

Firefighters' main fire-fighting tool is a pulaski, which has a hatchet blade for chopping on one side, and a hoe for digging up plants and clearing the ground on the other. They also wear hard hats and carry a first aid kit. A backpack contains water and equipment as well as any personal gear.

In case the fire gets out of control and changes direction suddenly, each firefighter also carries a fire shelter. This lifesaver is made of aluminum foil bonded onto fiberglass cloth. It reflects heat as intense as sixteen hundred degrees Fahrenheit while keeping the temperature inside the shelter no hotter than a dry sauna, about one hundred seventy degrees Fahrenheit. A firefighter can set up this low, triangular tent in under twenty seconds if necessary.

Dousing a Fire

Fires can also be slowed by dumping special fire-retardant chemicals on them. A typical mix contains: water; a chemical that helps put out the fire and later acts as a fertilizer for new growth; a thickening gum that makes the mixture thicker than molasses; and iron oxide, which gives it a red color. The color enables pilots to see where the retardant has already been dropped. The retardant helps slow the fire by smothering it with a layer that cuts down the availability of oxygen. It also reduces heat and adds moisture. When fires burn near lakes or rivers, helicopters carrying giant buckets can dip into the water, carry a hundred gallons of water to the fire, and dump it on the flames. Water fights fire by cooling the temperature of the potential fuel and cutting down on access to oxygen.

A plane releases fire retardant.

Smoke Jumpers

Most of western forest land is not accessible by roads. When forest managers decide to fight a fire in a remote area, they call in smoke jumpers, who parachute into the wilderness to do the job. These are highly trained firefighters. They must be able to get around, carrying heavy equipment, on the steepest mountain slopes, with no trails. They may have to work sixteen hours at a stretch, chopping down trees, pulling away brush, and digging into rocky ground.

A helicopter empties a water bucket on a fire.

Smoke jumpers are dropped in teams of two. For the jump, each wears a Kevlar jumpsuit for protection. The main parachute normally opens automatically, but each jumper has a smaller reserve chute, too. After landing, the jumpers pack away their jumpsuits and parachutes. Equipment such as shovels, pulaskis, saws, tree-climbing spurs, and sleeping bags are dropped in boxes from the plane, along with enough food and water for three days, the normal amount of time jumpers are expected to work on a fire. If they need to stay longer, more food and water can be dropped.

The first smoke jumpers went to work in 1940, in Idaho, from a base in Montana. Today, there are 350 to 400 smoke jumpers working out of eleven bases in the western United States. Becoming a smoke jumper isn't easy. Each agency with jumpers has its own requirements, but those of U.S. Forest Service (the government agency responsible for our national forests) Region One are typical. In order to apply, a person must be between 5 feet and 6 feet, 5 inches tall and weigh 120 to 200 pounds. He or she must be educated in the science of firefighting and have at least two years' experience as a firefighter in mountainous terrain.

In 1997, there were 120 applicants for two rookie openings. Those accepted for this region report for four weeks of training, along with rookies from other areas. Rookies must pass a physical fitness test right off the bat. Each must be able to do seven pull-ups, twenty-five push-ups, and forty-five sit-ups, and to run a mile and a half in less than eleven minutes. The first week of rookie training is brutal. Trainees get up at 4:30 A.M. to run two miles and do calisthenics before breakfast. Each must carry a pack weighing 110 pounds over a flat three-mile course in no more than ninety minutes and a pack weighing 85 pounds over two and a half miles of hilly, broken terrain in a reasonable amount of time. After passing these tests, the trainees spend the rest of the first week hacking at the ground with their pulaskis for sixteen hours at a time.

Those who survive the first week then learn additional skills including, how to jump from a plane, how to use ropes to get to the ground if they get hung up in the trees, and how to roll upon landing from a parachute jump. They must conquer a difficult obstacle course and also learn first aid and emergency procedures.

ABOVE: **The shock tower simulates the airplane that will deliver the jumpers.**
RIGHT: **Jumpers practice getting down from a tree on the hang-up simulator.**

52   In simulated jumps, each jumper is carried along a cable rather than using a parachute.

Experienced smoke jumpers take a break during their refresher course.

If a rookie fails to pass a test during any part of training, he or she is dropped from the program. At the end of training, each rookie must successfully complete seven parachute jumps. The first is into an open field, and the target gets smaller with each jump. The sixth is into the trees, and the seventh into water. Only those who are the most fit and determined make it through rookie camp to become smoke jumpers. Every year, returning jumpers must pass the same fitness test required of rookies, then go through two weeks of refresher training.

The training pays off. From 1940 to 1991, smoke jumpers completed more than 350,000 jumps. Only three resulted in death of the jumper. While the work is dangerous, smoke jumpers are rarely killed on the job. A dozen died in the famous Mann Gulch blaze in 1949, along with one other firefighter. In 1994, three smoke jumpers were among the fourteen firefighters who died when a Colorado fire overran them.

SIX

The fires of 1988, especially those in Yellowstone National Park, brought forest fires to the attention of the public. While the fires were raging, people worried that the park would be ruined forever. The photographs of forests aflame on the front pages of newspapers frightened readers, and stories about how firefighters couldn't control the blazes brought criticism.

The fires were inevitable. A lodgepole forest naturally burns every few hundred years, and most of Yellowstone's forests

For a while, it seemed as if all of Yellowstone was burning to the ground.

55

were just waiting for the right conditions. Really big fires had not hit Yellowstone since the 1700s, although some relatively large ones had burned in the 1800s. Yellowstone was just waiting to burn. The conditions in 1988 were so dry, and the moisture content of the trees was so low, that no one could stop the fires once they got underway.

Instead of merely burning the forest floor, the flames leapt into the tops of the trees, a phenomenon called crowning. Crowning results in canopy fires, which burn the branches that form the roof of the forest. The trees became giant torches. The intense heat whips up the wind, which then carries firebrands as far as two miles, starting still more fires.

Letting Fires Burn

For decades, fire was viewed as an enemy. Until 1972, any fire in a national forest or national park was fought. None were allowed to burn naturally. But over the years, scientists came to understand that fire did have a natural role in helping recycle the material in the forest, especially in the dry northern forests. In moist forests, bacteria, fungus, and insects help decompose dead trees and fallen leaves. But in dry forests, deadwood can lie on the forest floor for decades. As the years go by, more and more nutrients are locked up in both living trees and dead ones. Nutrients become harder and harder for growing trees to find, and the trees become less healthy. In addition, without fire, trees take over the grasslands that feed animals like elk and bison, because fires kill young trees at the meadow edges.

In 1972, a new fire policy was put in place for both national forests and national parks. Lightning fires that threatened private property or buildings would be fought, as would fires started by

When fire leaps to the crowns of the trees, nothing can stop it.

people. But lightning fires in certain areas would be left alone as long as they didn't become dangerous. In Yellowstone, the policy worked very well. From 1972 to 1987, 233 lightning fires were allowed to burn themselves out. Most of them—205—went out naturally after burning less than an acre, and none of the other 28 burned a very large area.

Yellowstone aflame.

The Fires of 1988

At first, the natural fires in 1988 were allowed to burn. The first started on June 14 in a national forest north of the park, but no one was worried. Enough rain normally falls in June and July to douse fires before they get very big. Fires started in the park, too,

Firefighters managed to save the Old Faithful Inn.

and most of them went out naturally, as in the past. But June had only 20 percent of its normal rainfall, and July began with sunny skies. By July 15, rain still hadn't fallen, and several fires had already burned about 8,000 acres of the park.

A week later, on July 21, the burned acreage had almost doubled, and park officials decided to fight all fires. However, high winds and dry conditions made their efforts almost hopeless. The North Fork Fire, for example, was smaller than 30 acres when reported, but grew to 500 acres in less than a day. Smoke jumpers, who had been sent in immediately, couldn't contain it.

As the hot, dry days rolled by, more and more of the forests burned. By August 12, more than 200,000 acres had been set aflame. Then, on August 20, hurricane-force gusts whipped up the fires, and 165,000 more acres burned in just one day.

Firefighters could do nothing to stop the fires, and it took all their efforts to keep them from destroying towns and park visitor areas. The historic Old Faithful Inn, built in 1903, was barely saved. Only when the first snow fell, on September 11, did the burning slow down, despite the $120 million spent on the desperate effort to stop the fires.

Aftermath

Despite the claims of television and newspaper reports, Yellowstone hadn't been destroyed by fire. Satellite images eventually showed that 793,880 acres of the 2.2 million acre park had burned. Many of the fires burned through the forests without killing all the trees. Other fires had burned through meadows and grasslands. And the forests that had been destroyed began to regrow with the first moisture in the fall.

Many people were worried about the animals in the park. It

Some of Yellowstone's forests were extensively burned in 1988.

turned out that fewer than three hundred of the thousands of large animals that live in the park died in the fire. Most of these were elk. By the time the fires became serious, most of the young birds had left their nests, so they could fly to escape the fire.

The ultimate result of the fires was a more varied landscape than before. Because the fires crowned in some areas and only

By 1989, the mosaic effect of living forests, dead trees, and meadows was easy to see.

burned the forest floor in others, a mosaic of patches of dead trees amid green forests was created. In some areas of the living forest, only the undergrowth burned, and others were completely untouched by the fire. This patchiness of the environment provided a richly varied habitat for Yellowstone's plants and animals, which allowed more species to live in a smaller area.

June 1989: Green plants were already growing again.

BACKGROUND: This forest near Tower Junction in Yellowstone was completely burned in 1988.

Fall 1994: Young shrubs were now growing thickly.

Spring 1997: A young lodgepole stands taller than the other plants, signaling the beginning of a new forest.

66 In 1989, visitors returned to Yellowstone and found the park's attractions, such as Old Faithful, just as fascinating as ever.

Continuing the Cycle

The greatest diversity of species should be found in Yellowstone's forests about twenty-five years after the fires, or around 2013. Fifteen to twenty-five years after that, the young lodgepoles will be tall enough to shade the forest floor thoroughly, and fewer kinds of plants and animals will be able to survive there.

When the new trees are one hundred to one hundred fifty years old, they will begin to die and fall, starting the buildup of fuel for the next round of fires. By the twenty-third century, the forests that now consist of thriving young pines will be overgrown, tangled, and old, like the forests of 1988. When the right conditions occur, the forests will burn once again.

SEVEN

HELPING NATURE WITH FIRE

Managers of some public lands now understand the importance of fire in the cycles of nature. When a lightning fire poses no danger to people or buildings, some public agencies now let it burn. Many forests that have not been allowed to burn for decades contain dangerous amounts of fuel. A lightning strike in such a forest could lead to a big, hot, dangerous fire. Suppressing fire in other environments, such as grasslands, has also led to undesirable changes. The best answer to these problems appears to be

Shrubs grow in the grassland in Aransas National Wildlife Refuge.

The controlled burn.

to fight fire with fire. Land managers use prescribed fire, carefully planned burns that bring about desirable changes.

Wildfires usually occur in the summer or early fall, when grasslands and forests are dry. But prescribed burning is more likely to be planned for less extreme conditions so the fires can be better controlled. For example, grassland burning at Aransas National Wildlife Refuge in Texas is done during the cool winter months. Prescribed burns in Montana forests are usually carried out during the spring.

Burning Forest Lands

The problems caused by fire suppression are huge. About 40 million acres of forests across the country are at risk for dangerous fires because natural fires have not been allowed to burn for so many years.

The goals of prescribed burning are clear. A prescribed fire should burn away heavy undergrowth of brush to remove potential fuel for wildfire. When a fire has plenty of fuel, it burns hotter and travels faster, covering more territory in less time and getting out of control more easily. With a moderate amount of fuel, a wildfire is less likely to burn hot enough to kill adult trees or to overrun an entire forest.

When the brush and deadwood on the forest floor burn, they release nutrients that can nourish the trees, grasses, and other forest plants. The less cluttered forest floor, with its fresh growth, provides fine habitat for wildlife such as elk and deer.

When the ground is barely cool, wild turkeys are already in the burned area looking for food.

Four months later, the shrubs are dead, and the grass is green.

The increase in food for wildlife brought about by burning can also be dramatic. When shrubs are allowed to grow without fire, more and more energy goes into maintaining the old wood, and less goes into new growth. When the old wood burns, the shrub puts out many new, succulent shoots that provide food for deer and elk. In an acre of northern shrubland deprived of fire for twenty years, only thirty to forty-five pounds of food for wildlife is produced yearly. After a fire, that same acre will produce at least four hundred to six hundred pounds of food in a year.

Deciding to Burn

How do land managers decide where to burn? Hundreds of thousands of acres of public lands are possible candidates. In recent years, more and more people have moved into the countryside, often right on the borders of National Forest lands. Such areas are at the top of the list for prescribed burns so that the fire hazard to people and homes is reduced.

Controlled burning in a California forest.

In 1997, the U.S. Forest Service decided to burn more than 52,000 acres in its Northern Region (Montana and parts of Idaho, North Dakota, South Dakota, and Wyoming). Five million acres of northern forests evolved over the ages with fire and were burned by lightning fires about every twenty years. Such forests consisted mostly of ponderosa pines, with some larch and Douglas fir. The frequent, natural fires burned low to the ground, killing the underbrush and young firs, which produced an open forest.

More than eighty years of fire suppression has changed these forests dramatically. Now they are overcrowded with Douglas fir and prone to superhot fires that can kill older trees and sterilize the soil, making regrowth take years longer. Such hot, intense fires are also more dangerous to firefighters.

Unfortunately, many of the forests have gone so long without fire that even prescribed burning would be dangerous. Some logging or thinning of the trees would need to be done before they can be safely burned.

ABOVE: Lighting a burn in Montana.
BELOW: Controlled burns are carefully watched and tended. Note that this firefighter carries all his usual equipment, including his emergency shelter in the yellow pack, just in case.

Restoring Grasslands

Native Americans once helped maintain healthy grasslands with their fires. Now managers of wildlands are doing the same thing in many parts of the country. An example is the Buenos Aires National Wildlife Refuge south of Tucson, Arizona. This refuge represents the last remnant of Sonoran savanna grasslands in the United States. Cattle once roamed across the refuge, feeding on the grasses and changing the ecosystem drastically.

Now, cattle have been barred, and the refuge is burned to get rid of weeds and shrubs like mesquite. The endangered masked bobwhite quail is being reintroduced, and habitat is being created for birds that stop there on their long migrations.

Critics Have Their Say

Not everyone is happy with prescribed burning. Cattle ranchers would like to return their herds to the Buenos Aires refuge, and many critics complain about the cost of reintroducing quail.

Prescribed fire in forests also has its opponents. Some believe logging can solve the problem of crowded forests, while others fear that fires will escape into populated areas. But the problem of lands damaged by leaving out fire, a major player in the natural system, will not go away. One way or another, fire will take part. A controlled burn costs money and can cause some air pollution. But fighting a wildfire is many more times as expensive and can bring long periods of smoky conditions. Controlled burns are good "preventative medicine" and can help fire return to its role of maintaining and renewing ecosystems.

Fires can cause serious air pollution.

Index

Page numbers in *italics* refer to illustrations.